More
Why do we say that?

More
Why do we say that?

MORE WHY DO WE SAY THAT?

Graham Donaldson & Maris Ross

Illustrations by Larry

DAVID & CHARLES
Newton Abbot   London

British Library Cataloguing In Publication Data

Donaldson, Graham
  More why do we say that?
  1. Sayings in English – Anthologies
  I. Title II. Ross, Maris
  398′.9′21

  ISBN 0 7153 9444 4

Typeset by Typesetters (Birmingham) Ltd,
Smethwick, West Midlands
and printed in Great Britain

for David & Charles Publishers plc
Brunel House Newton Abbot Devon

CONTENTS

WHY DO WE SAY . . .

STEAL HIS THUNDER

Stealing someone's thunder means to take glory or attention away from him. John Dennis, a seventeenth-century English dramatist, was the first man literally to have his thunder stolen.

For his play *Appius and Virginia*, he invented a new sound effects device to reproduce thunder, filling the auditorium with a loud rumble from a gadget that looked like a wooden trough. But audiences did not like the play and the management of the Drury Lane Theatre brought the curtain down after a very short run and staged Shakespeare's *Macbeth* instead.

When a roll of thunder sounded at the appropriate scene in *Macbeth*, Dennis complained, 'That is my thunder, by God! The villains will play my thunder, but not my plays.'

Alas for him, he wrote more unsuccessful plays than successful ones but was better remembered as a critic.

WHY DO WE SAY ...

WIN ONE'S SPURS

When someone gains recognition in a sphere of achievement, he wins his spurs just as knights did in the medieval days of chivalry.

Under the codes of chivalry, a young nobleman began his training as a squire and wore silver spurs with which to urge on his horse. When he had shown sufficient valour to be dubbed a knight, he was ceremoniously tapped on the shoulder with a sword and also presented with a pair of gilt spurs to mark his elevation.

Several particularly fierce combats in the Middle Ages were called the Battle of the Spurs because of the huge number of gilt spurs found lying on the battlefield after the carnage.

WHY DO WE SAY . . .

TURN A BLIND EYE

Viscount Horatio Nelson, Britain's most famous naval hero, was responsible for 'turning a blind eye', meaning that he ignored an event.

At the naval battle of Copenhagen in 1801, Nelson was subordinate to Sir Hyde Parker, who hoisted the flag signalling the British ships to withdraw as he felt Danish resistance was stronger than expected.

'Now damn me if I do,' Nelson said. 'I have a right to be blind sometimes.' He put his spyglass to his right eye, whose sight he had lost from shell fragments seven years earlier. Then he added, 'I really do not see the signal.'

He carried on the fight instead of retreating, and the Danish ships ended up surrendering.

WHY DO WE SAY ...

GO HAYWIRE

If someone goes haywire, they act in a crazy or disorganised way. The saying dates back to the early logging days in the forests of New England when the timber was hauled out by teams of horses or mules.

The animals were fed on bales of hay which were held together by wire. In a dilapidated or poorly equipped logging camp, the wire from the eaten bales would then be used to hold various bits of equipment together. The loggers would contemptuously call that type of camp a 'haywire outfit'.

LAUGH UP YOUR SLEEVE

If you have secret grounds for amusement, you laugh up your sleeve. This was exactly what people used to do centuries ago.

In the Middle Ages, sleeves were very wide. If you wanted to enjoy a private joke, you could raise your arm and use the sleeve to screen your face. By the sixteenth century, sleeves became narrower but people still spoke of laughing up their sleeve.

WHY DO WE SAY ...

TOUCH AND GO

There you are, driving along, when suddenly another car pulls out and misses you by a fraction. It was a narrow escape, touch and go whether you would avoid an accident.

Sailors originally used 'touch and go' to describe any risky venture. Admiral William Smyth, who wrote the *Sailors' Word Book* in 1867, said it meant 'anything within an ace of ruin, as in rounding a ship very narrowly to escape rocks, or when, under sail, she rubs against the ground with her keel.'

The phrase could have started from the way the old sailing barges manoeuvred on the River Thames. They negotiated the channel by changing tack each time they touched bottom on the other side – very much touch and go, with the risk of getting stuck on the mud banks.

WHY DO WE SAY ...

ON TENTERHOOKS

A good book or drama will keep you on tenterhooks, in a state of tension or suspense about the outcome.

The phrase comes from the days before textile mills, when cloth was stretched on wooden frames called tenters. Bent nails were set around the frame as the hooks on which to stretch the fabric. These tenter hooks got their name from the Latin verb to stretch, *tendere*, and were useful for hanging other objects, like carcasses of meat.

WHY DO WE SAY ...

AUNT SALLY

Poor Aunt Sally, she is set up as the target of unreasonable attack.

She got her name in the nineteenth century at fairs and race meetings where the figure of a woman's head, with a pipe in its mouth, was set up as a variation of the game of skittles. The player had to break the pipe by throwing sticks at 'Aunt Sally'.

By the end of the century, Aunt Sally meant anyone who became the victim of unjustified criticism.

WHY DO WE SAY ...

HOIST WITH HIS OWN PETARD

A person hoist with his own petard has become the victim of his own scheme. He sets out to injure someone else but the plan backfires and traps him instead.

A petard was a siege weapon in the sixteenth and seventeenth centuries. Gun powder was put in a metal or wooden box and used to blow a hole in the weak point of fortifications. But the contraption was so erratic that whoever lit the fuse risked blowing themselves up.

Shakespeare was alive when the petard was in use. In *Hamlet*, he portrays Polonius, who wants to trap Hamlet, as hoist with his own petard.

WHY DO WE SAY ...

PIN MONEY

A woman who wants to save or earn a little money for incidental expenses will call it her pin money.

In the sixteenth century when husbands had absolute control of the purse strings, wives started asking for a small sum to buy the handy new invention of pins so they could secure their hair, hat or shawl. From buying a few pins, women stretched their 'pin money' into a dress allowance or for buying other incidentals.

WHY DO WE SAY ...

SLEEP LIKE A TOP

The wooden spinning top is one of the oldest of toys, an unlikely source of comparison with anyone who enjoys a deep sleep.

But the people of medieval times were fascinated by the toy. They noticed that when it spun round fast enough, perfectly balanced on its point, the top appeared not to move. They joked that the top was asleep. As far back as 1616, sound sleepers were therefore described as 'sleeping like a top'.

WHY DO WE SAY ...

BOB'S YOUR UNCLE

All you have to do is one simple action and Bob's your uncle! You have attained something very easily.

Just like Arthur Balfour did in 1886. Lord Salisbury, the British Prime Minister, appointed Arthur to an important government post. Many considered the appointment was not made on merit but because 'Bob was his uncle'. He was the nephew of Lord Salisbury, whose Christian name was Robert, or Bob for short.

In fact Mr Balfour proved a formidable politician and later became Prime Minister himself.

WHY DO WE SAY ...

TO BLACKBALL SOMEONE

When someone is blackballed, they are ostracised by society. The term harks back to the heyday of gentlemen's clubs in the eighteenth and nineteenth centuries.

Entry into venerable institutions like the Athenaeum in London depended on the vote of one's fellows as to eligibility. The ballot was an anonymous one. If the existing members agreed with the suitability of an applicant, they put a white wooden or ivory ball in the voting box. If they wanted to shun the applicant, they signified their negative vote with a black ball.

WHY DO WE SAY ...

THE BITTER END

When you have finally completed an undertaking, no matter how difficult or unpleasant, you have seen it through to the bitter end.

This saying goes back four centuries to the days of sailing ships and had nothing to do with the sailors getting angry. Bitts were strong posts fastened on the deck of a ship for securing the anchor and other cables. When the rope was paid out to the bitter end, that was as far as it could go. Thus, when you have reached the bitter end, you cannot go any further.

Incidentally, a ship's posts for securing mooring lines and other cables are still called bitts today.

WHY DO WE SAY ...

TO STONEWALL

The stonewaller is well known in politics, business and cricket. He stands unmoved, resolute in his defensive efforts to thwart the proceedings.

The name goes back to a Confederate general in the American civil war, Thomas Jonathan Jackson, and his defence at the Battle of Bull Run in 1861. Someone in the heat of the fight was heard to shout, 'Look, there's Jackson standing like a stone wall.' His troops promptly became known as the Stonewall Brigade and the nickname stuck with the general.

A sad footnote: Stonewall Jackson was accidentally shot and killed by his own side in another battle two years later.

WHY DO WE SAY ...

BUSMAN'S HOLIDAY

So, you're on a busman's holiday, spending your free time doing much the same thing as you do at work.

A few drivers of the old horse buses liked their animals so much that they spent their days off as passengers on their own buses, to check that the relief driver treated their teams all right. The horse bus reached its peak in London in 1901 when almost 4,000 of them were in service.

WHY DO WE SAY ...

PYRRHIC VICTORY

At times victory can be a costly affair, with the winner no better off than the loser. The First World War contained many examples of Pyrrhic victories when long, bloody battles achieved little while thousands died on both sides.

King Pyrrhus, a land-hungry warrior who ruled part of Greece from the age of twelve, would have been at home on these battlefields. In the third century BC he set out to conquer Italy. After winning the Battle of Asculum in 279 BC by sacrificing some of his best troops, he is supposed to have said, 'One more such victory and we are lost.' So, a Pyrrhic victory is one where the cost is too high.

WHY DO WE SAY ...

GONE FOR A BURTON

Something that is broken or lost is said to have gone for a Burton. The saying comes from a 1940s advertising campaign by an English brewery, Burton Ales in Staffordshire.

Their posters showed well-known groups of people with one obvious person missing and the words: 'He's gone for a Burton'. With typical dry humour, World War II pilots in Britain adopted the phrase for the fate of airmen who failed to return.

WHY DO WE SAY . . .

HOBSON'S CHOICE

When you have no choice at all, this is known as Hobson's choice. Back in the seventeenth century, Hobson was a carrier of goods and packages in the English university town of Cambridge. He also hired out horses. But customers were never allowed to pick and choose.

If they wanted one of Mr Hobson's horses, they had to take the one standing nearest the stable door or none at all. So they had Hobson's choice – or nothing.

Despite this idiosyncrasy, Hobson was a valued citizen. He helped to provide Cambridge with a badly needed clean water supply in 1606. To this day he is still remembered with a street, a fountain and a stream named after him.

WHY DO WE SAY ...

PEEPING TOM

Society hates a Peeping Tom, a voyeur who furtively pries on scenes that are none of his business. The original Peeping Tom was a tailor when Lady Godiva made her famous ride naked through the English town of Coventry in the eleventh century.

Lady Godiva was the wife of Leofric, Earl of Mercia, whose domain included Coventry. Exasperated by her pleas to reduce the town's taxes, he agreed to do so only if she rode naked through the market place. She dumbfounded him by doing so. By way of thanks, the townspeople saved her blushes by staying indoors and closing their shutters.

All, that is, except Tom the Tailor. To his disgrace, he peeped. The story goes that he was struck blind for his wickedness.

WHY DO WE SAY ...

TEDDY BEAR

The teddy bear is the favourite toy of millions of children. When they grow up, Teddy is still remembered with affection and even passed on to children's children. But how did he get his name?

Oddly enough, an American president is responsible. Theodore Roosevelt, whose nickname was Teddy, was invited on a hunting trip in Mississippi in 1903. His host, wishing to ensure that the President bagged something, caught and stunned a small bear and left it at a pre-arranged spot. Roosevelt, however, discovered the trick and would have nothing to do with it.

When the story emerged, the *Washington Post* published a cartoon of the scene. This was too good an opportunity for toy manufacturers to miss. They immediately renamed their line in cuddly stuffed bears as teddy bears.

WHY DO WE SAY ...

RUNNING THE GAUNTLET

An unpopular politician could soon tell you what running the gauntlet means today: to be attacked on all sides.

He would expect only a verbal onslaught but running the gauntlet used to be physical punishment, first used in Sweden where *lopp* meant running and *gata* meant lane, anglicised into gauntlet.

The British Navy adopted the punishment in 1661. Theft was abhorred aboard ship and the culprit was made to run between two lines of sailors each armed with a rope. The Royal Navy abolished the practice in 1813 but it lingered on in public schools where offenders had to run between rows of boys striking out with fists or wet towels.

WHY DO WE SAY ...

CAN'T HOLD A CANDLE TO HIM

Soccer fans discussing their heroes might well say, 'Smith? He can't hold a candle to Jones.' This means the talent of Smith is nowhere near that of Jones.

The saying goes back to the seventeenth century when link-boys carried torches to show travellers along London's streets after dark. They hired themselves out by crying, 'Have a light, gentlemen?' The task did not require much intelligence and was a very subordinate position. So, if you wanted to insult someone, you would say, 'He's not fit to hold a candle to anyone.'

WHY DO WE SAY ...

THE ACID TEST

In the eighteenth and nineteenth centuries, a crude but certain way of testing whether gold was real or fake was to see if it withstood the highly corrosive effect of aquafortis, as nitric acid was then called.

Nitric acid dissolves most metals but gold is an exception. So if a sample withstood aquafortis, it had passed the original acid test. Being colourless, it bore the Latin name for strong water. Today's methods for testing gold are far more refined, but the acid test survives to mean any crucial test.

WHY DO WE SAY ...

GET OUT OF BED
ON THE WRONG SIDE

You know the feeling when everything seems wrong. You are moody and cross. Someone is bound to tell you that you got out of bed on the wrong side.

The wrong side is the left, associated with bad luck in old superstitions because the devil lived on the left side of God before being banished. The right side is therefore considered the lucky side, so if you 'put your best foot forward,' it is the right foot. That is the side to favour, if you want the spirits to smile on you.

WHY DO WE SAY ...

RAINING CATS AND DOGS

It may seem odd to associate cats and dogs with a downpour of rain and raging winds. But there's good reason.

First the cats: They were the devil's animal in folk belief and were thought to have power over good and evil. That power extended to control over the weather. The superstitious believed that if a cat washed its face, that meant rain. If seen leaping or clawing, that was an omen of gales.

Now the dogs: Odin was a Viking god and his attendant was a dog, which symbolized the wind.

When we have torrential rain, it's therefore raining cats and dogs.

WHY DO WE SAY ...

THE REAL McCOY

'Now *that* is the real McCoy', a connoisseur might say when he comes across the genuine article.

The saying could have originated in Scotland around 1870 when a whisky distiller called G. Mackay promoted his whisky as 'the real Mackay' to distinguish it from a rival company also called Mackay.

Then 'Kid' McCoy, an American prize fighter in the 1890s, liked to boast that someone in a bar challenged him to prove his identity. So McCoy knocked the unfortunate person out and when he came round, he agreed, 'You're the real McCoy!'

Equally colourful is the story of Bill McCoy, who smuggled whisky from Canada into the United States during the prohibition era. He was proud to claim his whisky was 'the real McCoy', not home distilled.

WHY DO WE SAY . . .

A LOAD OF BUNKUM

It had to be a politician who invented this saying! His name was Felix
Walker, an American congressman who represented Buncombe
County in North Carolina.

He surpassed himself for talking rubbish during a debate in the
House of Representatives in the 1820s. When taken to task for time
wasting, he said, 'I was not speaking to the House, but to Buncombe.'
This evolved into talking a load of bunkum or bunk whenever anyone
speaks a lot of nonsense.

MAROONED
SHIP
IN
VIEW

THE DEVIL TO PAY

In the days of wooden ships, the devil was the name for the longest seam of the hull. Every so often it had to be caulked or 'paid', an awkward job as the vessel had to be tipped on its side between tides.

The seam was then sealed with hot pitch. Serious trouble loomed, as the phrase now means, when sailors had 'the devil to pay and no pitch hot', to use the full phrase.

WHY DO WE SAY ...

POSH PEOPLE

They are the people who live in style, doing the right things and going to the right places. And it was part of that lifestyle which created the term posh.

In the days of the British Empire, experienced travellers going by steamship to India booked their cabins port side out, starboard home – POSH for short – so that in each direction they would be on the cooler side of the ship, sheltered from the sun.

WHY DO WE SAY . . .

ALWAYS RESERVED FOR MONSIEUR BENNETT

GORDON BENNETT

Who was he, this man whose name we use when we are told something remarkable, extraordinary, amazing? Well, he was remarkable, extraordinary and amazing.

For instance, he was the man who despatched Henry Stanley to deepest Africa in 1871 to find Dr Livingstone, no expense spared. As editor of the *New York Herald*, he was such a lavish spender that he was reputed to have spent thirty million dollars of the newspaper's revenue on such ventures. Another of his amazing scoops was the news that General Custer and his men had been massacred by Indians.

He established the Paris edition of the *New York Herald* in 1887. His high spending continued there. When he could not get a table in a busy restaurant, he bought the place so that he could sit down to mutton chops. Then he told a waiter that he could keep the restaurant on condition that chips were always on the menu and that a table was always available for Gordon Bennett. What more can one say than . . . Gordon Bennett!

WHY DO WE SAY ...

THE COLD SHOULDER

You know when you are being given the cold shoulder. You are ignored, frozen out, made to feel unwelcome.

In days of old, the cold shoulder was literally given to guests who had outstayed their welcome. If the host felt the guest had lingered for too many days of wining and dining, along came the big hint. The cold leftovers of lamb, normally fit only for servants, would be served on a plate. Exit guest.

WHY DO WE SAY . . .

IN THE DOGHOUSE

You have got to be a bit of a saint not to have spent some time in the doghouse. It means that you are in disgrace.

The first person to be sent 'to the doghouse' was Mr Darling in *Peter Pan*, the ever popular children's play written by Sir James Matthew Barrie in 1904. Mr Darling, the children's father, is beastly to Nana, their dog, and chains it up outside. As his punishment, he lives in the doghouse until the children come home from their adventures.

WHY DO WE SAY ...

ACHILLES' HEEL

An Achilles' heel is a small but fatal weakness, the one that killed the legendary hero of Greek mythology.

Achilles was the son of the sea goddess Thetis, who dipped him into the River Styx as a child to make him invincible. The one part she forgot to dip was his heel because she was holding him by the ankle.

As a warrior in the Trojan Wars, Achilles' body was invulnerable until he was fatally wounded by an arrow in the heel which struck his one weak point.

Why do we say . . .

St. Louis Herald
MISSISSIPPI MISHAP
BOAT HITS SNAG

Hit a snag

Life seldom runs smoothly. Suddenly a problem rears its head. Things have hit a snag.

Why a snag? This word is Scandinavian in origin and meant spike or jagged projection. Migrants took the word to America where it was a common comment on the river boats when they hit a tree stump hidden in the water.

Gradually the word took on a wider meaning. In 1886, the London *Pall Mall Gazette* said, 'Our extradition treaty with the United States has run up against its first snag, to use an expression familiar on the Mississippi.'

WHY DO WE SAY ...

BORN WITH A SILVER SPOON IN HIS MOUTH

If people think someone has always been very rich, they will say he was born with a silver spoon in his mouth.

The saying goes back to the sixteenth and seventeenth centuries when it was customary for godchildren of wealthy families to be given sets of silver spoons as christening presents. Silver remains a traditional christening present among those who can afford it, though the baby of rich parents is far less likely to be fed with a silver spoon these days.

Why do we say . . .

A COCK-AND-BULL STORY

In the heyday of travel by coach and horses, the Cock and the Bull were two flourishing English inns that stood side by side on the main road fifty miles north of London.

The London-bound coaches pulled into one inn and the outward-bound coaches stopped at the other to change teams of horses and, naturally enough, bring news from their towns of origin. The gossip grew more exaggerated in bouncing back and forth between inn customers.

The tales were so outlandish that any incredible or misleading yarn was labelled a cock-and-bull story. The inn buildings still exist in Stony Stratford, now part of the new city of Milton Keynes, but the coaches stopped calling when the railways were built in the nineteenth century.

WHY DO WE SAY ...

THAT'S CLAPTRAP

Quiz show presenters are the masters of claptrap these days. When they introduce a contestant and pause for the audience to clap after naming his home town or occupation, they have set a trap to win applause. That's claptrap.

The phrase came from the theatre in the eighteenth century when actors set up showy, sentimental expressions particularly designed to win applause. They even developed mechanical clappers to add to the atmosphere. But the expressions came to be recognised as rubbish. That is what claptrap means today, a lot of nonsense.

WHY DO WE SAY . . .

PICK YOUR OWN BLACKBERRIES

FALL GUY

The fall guy takes the blame. His rough time began in the 1920s when rigged wrestling matches became common in the United States.

He would agree to participate in a match and take a prearranged 'fall' to make the prize wrestler look good. The phrase took on the connotation of being deceived into taking the rap, because the fall guy was often badly beaten up instead of getting the promised light treatment from his victorious opponent.

WHY DO WE SAY ...

BY HOOK OR BY CROOK

Hook and crook were medieval reaping tools, the curved billhook with its sharp edge for cutting and the crook for holding the corn while it was cut.

The story goes that King William Rufus of England was slain by an arrow in the back on a hunting expedition in the New Forest in 1100. His brother, Henry, rode off to claim the throne. Sir Walter Tyrrel, who fired the arrow, fled to France, and the others in the hunting party dispersed, leaving the body lying on the ground. A charcoal burner named Purkiss was the one who found the body of the disliked tyrant and took it for burial. As his reward, he won the right to gather firewood that he could reach with his hook and crook.

It was hardly the easiest way to collect wood but guaranteed that the trees would be pruned instead of felled, and peasants were not normally allowed to cut firewood in the king's hunting forest. By hook or by crook now means to achieve something by all means fair or foul.

WHY DO WE SAY ...

THAT'S MY BUGBEAR

What a bugbear! You might well say that when a problem causes anxiety or dread.

Bwg, pronounced bug, is the Welsh word for ghost or hobgoblin. Of course, a bear is a pretty frightening creature. Join the two together as they did in the sixteenth century, and a make-believe monster is created to carry children away if they are naughty. Down the years, the disciplinarians of the nursery also used bogeymen, bogles and bug-a-boos, all mischievous spirits from the same origin, to frighten children into good behaviour.

WHY DO WE SAY . . .

CURATE'S EGG

A curate's egg is a mixed blessing, good in parts, bad in others.

The description is almost a hundred years old and comes from a cartoon that set a lot of clergymen laughing in sympathy when published in 1895 in the weekly *Punch* magazine in London. The assistant to an Anglican bishop used to be called a curate and he was obviously not in a position to cross his senior. In the cartoon, an unfortunate curate is dining with his bishop, who says, 'I'm afraid you've got a bad egg, Mr Jones.' The curate tactfully replies, 'Oh no, my lord, I assure you parts of it are excellent.'

WHY DO WE SAY ...

HAMMER AND TONGS

A couple going for each other 'hammer and tongs' are quarreling with all the energy at their command. The phrase harks back to the days when a blacksmith made all sorts of metal objects in addition to horse shoes.

He took the hot metal straight from the forge, holding it steady with tongs in one hand while beating it into shape with a hammer in the other. He always had to work as quickly as possible before the iron cooled and was no longer malleable. Anyone who pursues a target with all the force at their command therefore came to be known as going at it hammer and tongs.

WHY DO WE SAY ...

PLEASED AS PUNCH

Someone pleased as Punch could not be more proud of themselves, just like the puppet in the popular old show.

An Italian actor began the character under the name of Pulcinella or Punchinello in the seventeenth century and it was taken up by puppeteers all over Europe. They played 'Punch and Judy' shows at fairs and entertainment booths at the seaside and still do so occasionally today as children's entertainment.

The glove puppet of Punch usually appears as grotesque and hump-backed with a large red nose. Yet he is very pleased with himself as he clowns around, performing dreadful deeds like beating his wife Judy and dropping the baby. Anything particularly outrageous is accompanied by his insincere comment, 'What a pity!'

WHY DO WE SAY . . .

CHEW THE FAT

To chew the fat means to talk a long time, usually in a grumbling way over some grievance, which is exactly what sailors used to do about the food aboard ship.

The old way of preserving meat was to pack it in barrels of brine, and salt beef was one of the few staples that could last through a long voyage. But the salt curing process made the beef very tough. The seamen had to chew endlessly to swallow the unpalatable and fatty meat down. At least it gave them an off duty chance to chat, usually grumbling that 'God made the vittles but the devil made the cook.'

WHY DO WE SAY ...

LEFT IN THE LURCH

A person abandoned in a position of great difficulty is left in the lurch. The saying goes all the way back to the sixteenth century when 'lurch' meant a swindle.

So its origin could have come from the victim of the swindle, abandoned by those who had hoodwinked him and left in the lurch.

At the same time, lurch was the word used to denote a particular score at the end of various card games such as whist, when the winner was well ahead of the others. The losers were certainly left in a difficult situation because the winner had 'lurched' or left them far behind.

WHY DO WE SAY ...

LICK INTO SHAPE

Unlikely as it sounds in today's state of knowledge, our ancestors believed certain animals were born formless and their mothers licked them into shape.

This false notion especially applied in the fifteenth century to bears, fiercely protective creatures which did not allow humans near their young. All the distant observer could see was the large bear licking a bundle of fur.

In fact she was cleaning her cub. Appropriately the saying 'lick into shape' now means making something presentable or moulding it into a system.

WHY DO WE SAY ...

COCK A SNOOK

When you cock a snook at someone, you are showing contempt for them.

Snooks was an old word for the derisive gesture of placing a thumb on the nose. English street urchins of the nineteenth century would complete their show of derision for authority by cocking, or lifting, their nose upwards. Their other saucy trick was to put their tongue in their cheek.

Eventually the phrase meant showing contempt whether or not the gesture was actually performed.

WHY DO WE SAY ...

IN QUARANTINE

Quarantine means exclusion from the company of others and comes from the Latin word for forty.

Quarantine was especially applied to sailing ships when it was realized that travellers spread contagious diseases. The original number of days of isolation imposed on a ship was forty before those aboard could enter port and mix with the inhabitants.

For English noblewomen in the seventeenth and eighteenth centuries, quarantine held another meaning. When their husbands died, some widows had to remove from the main mansion of the estate to a smaller 'dower' house while the larger home passed to the heir of the next generation. But for forty days, known as the widow's quarantine, a woman could remain in her late husband's mansion.

WHY DO WE SAY ...

HAM ACTOR

A ham actor is a truly dreadful one whose performance is so shallow or over-played that the audience deride him. The term arose within the theatrical profession when the full slang word for incompetence on stage was 'hamfatter'.

Theatre flourished as popular entertainment in nineteenth century America but money was often short and the cheapest way to remove greasepaint make-up was by using the fat from ham. The verdict of contempt for a fellow actor therefore was to call him a hamfatter.

WHY DO WE SAY . . .

USING YOUR LOAF

The Cockneys, or East Enders of London, are famous for their rhyming slang. Using your loaf, meaning to use your common sense, rhymes loaf of bread with head.

But it also rhymes with dead, and the first use of the phrase was in the trenches of World War I when 'Duck your loaf' was the terse Cockney instruction to keep your head below the trench or end up dead. Between the wars, Cockney sergeants started saying 'use your loaf' to chivvy recruits who were slow at following orders.

WHY DO WE SAY ...

COLD ENOUGH TO FREEZE THE BALLS OFF A BRASS MONKEY

This is not as rude as it sounds. A brass or iron monkey was a type of cannon in the seventeenth century.

The cannon balls were stacked in pyramids but if it was cold enough, the pyramids tumbled over because the iron balls contracted more quickly than the brass trays in which they were stacked.

So if it's cold enough to freeze the balls off a brass monkey, the weather is extreme.

WHY DO WE SAY ...

THROW IN THE SPONGE

In the prize fights of the nineteenth century, the sponge used to wipe the contestants' faces would be thrown in the air, signalling that it would not be needed any more, when one of the contestants wanted to surrender.

Nowadays we talk of throwing in the sponge to mean giving up or surrendering. In boxing, a towel is still thrown into the ring by the second to signal that the fighter is giving up.

WHY DO WE SAY ...

MIND YOUR Ps AND Qs

People who mind their Ps and Qs are careful about their behaviour, a far cry from the unruly waterfront bars where sailors used to drink.

Some inn keepers would give them credit until payday, chalking up on a slate how many pints and quarts they had ordered, abbreviated to P and Q. They had to mind their Ps and Qs to keep the record straight.

By the nineteenth century, children were admonished to mind their Ps and Qs but teachers did not mention the lowly origins. The more genteel explanation was that the letter p was easy to muddle with q.

WHY DO WE SAY ...

PIPE DOWN

Orders are still piped in the navy, harking back to when they were whistled by the boatswain. The last pipe of the day on a warship is called the pipe down.

This signals the order for silence and lights to be dimmed so that sailors not keeping the night watch can sleep. The phrase came ashore as a way to ask people to stop making a noise.

WHY DO WE SAY ...

TILT AT WINDMILLS

In that classic of western literature, the self-appointed knight errant Don Quixote mistakes an array of windmills for giants whom he must slay.

He charges the first windmill but his lance gets entangled and he is spun round by the sail until he falls back to earth. Miguel de Cervantes intended the adventures of his elderly knight to be a satire on chivalry, prevalent when he wrote the book in 1605.

The allusion to windmills has stayed with us as meaning to attack imaginary or impractical foes.

WHY DO WE SAY . . .

QUIZ

Mr Daly, the manager of a Dublin theatre in the 1780s, laid a bet that he could introduce a new and meaningless word into the English language within twenty-four hours.

He chalked the word QUIZ on various walls within public view and, sure enough, within twenty-four hours Dubliners were inquiring what quiz meant. Mr Daly may also have known some Latin because *quis* means 'who' or 'what' in Latin.

After his escapade, it came to mean questioning, though in his era it also signified a practical joke or eccentric person. Little did he know the quiz games that were to follow on radio and television.

WHY DO WE SAY ...

HOLD THE FORT

During the American civil war, Union General John Murray Corse was attacked by the Confederates at Allatoona Pass in 1864. General William Sherman sent him a signal saying, 'Hold the fort. I am coming.'

Corse gallantly fought on, and Sherman's phrase passed into language, popularised in a hymn and in literature. It now means to keep things going or take temporary charge.

WHY DO WE SAY ...

GONE TO POT

A person or institution gone to pot has been neglected beyond the point of salvation. The saying alludes to the days when broken items of gold and silver were thrown back into the melting pot if considered beyond repair.

The metal from stolen jewellery met the same fate, so that it could not be identified.

Gone to the dogs had the same meaning of ruin from the sixteenth century, when the leftovers that nobody else wanted were thrown to the dogs. Then as now, it was also abusive to compare a man with a dog.

WHY DO WE SAY . . .

PARTING SHOT

The horsemen of Parthia had a real battle to keep the Roman Empire
from encroaching on their ancient kingdom in western Asia, now part
of Iran. They had a particular trick of firing their arrows backwards
while pretending to be in flight.

This manoeuvre, the Parthian shot, staved off the Romans.
Anglicised as 'the parting shot', it is now taken as having the final and
most effective word in a debate.

WHY DO WE SAY . . .

SWAN SONG

The ancient Greeks believed that the soul of Apollo, their god of music, passed into a swan and that because of this every swan sang beautifully just before it died.

Although the idea was false, great names of literature such as Chaucer, Shakespeare and Tennyson took up the theme. Swan song came to mean the last work of a composer, poet or actor before his death or retirement.

WHY DO WE SAY ...

PLAY POSSUM

The furry little opossum feigns death when it is threatened or attacked. No other creature plays death quite so well, lying limply on its side with its tongue hanging out and eyes shut.

Slave owners in America's deep south who suspected slaves of shamming sickness to avoid work would claim he was 'coming possum over us'. The slave trade came to an end, but playing possum survived as meaning to pretend illness or death.

WHY DO WE SAY ...

GET DOWN TO BRASS TACKS

Choosing the right fabric was a lengthy business of looking at rolls in the old-fashioned draper's shop. When you had finally decided which one you wanted, you got down to brass tacks.

The brass tacks or nails were hammered at one yard intervals along the counter and the shopkeeper measured out how many yards of material you wanted. The nails were later replaced by measuring rules, but getting down to brass tacks still means to be practical or to get down to basics.

WHY DO WE SAY ...

PIE IN THE SKY

Joe Hill, an early American union leader, wrote a song which warned workers not to be exploited by their employers. 'You'll get pie in the sky when you die,' he said.

At that time, pie was associated with wealth because it was a slang word for treat, like the rewards drawn from bran pie, the old name for dipping for hidden prizes in the bran tub. His song turned the phrase into meaning false promises, utopian dreams that are never realized.

Hill belonged to a labour organisation, the Industrial Workers of the World, which was very radical. He was executed in 1915 on a murder charge which his associates said was trumped up in order to get rid of the unrest he caused. Just before his death, he said, 'Don't waste any time in mourning. Organise.'

WHY DO WE SAY ...

RED LETTER DAY

Five centuries ago, ecclesiastical calendars started using red pigment on parchment to denote saints' days and church festivals among the black lettering of other days.

They came to be associated with memorable events, often signifying a day off and celebration at a fair. A red letter day is still synonymous with a happy special occasion.

WHY DO WE SAY ...

GRASS WIDOW

The wives of officers serving in India during the days of British colonial rule stayed up in the cool of the hill stations while their husbands served through the worst heat on the hot dusty plains.

They were called grass widows, not because the grass grew on the cooler heights but from the idea of being sent away on holiday or turned out to grass, as horses were sent to pasture after work. Thus, by the mid-1850s, a grass widow signified a married woman whose husband was temporarily absent.

MOONLIGHTING

By the light of the moon, various people used to engage on illicit acts. In Ireland, gangs of men acting for landlords were called moonlighters when they attacked tenants to try to force them out.

Much more recently, moonlighting has come to mean doing a second paid job, usually at night, on top of holding down a steady job by day.

WHY DO WE SAY...

CRY WOLF

In all the different versions of a very old fable, the shepherd boy keeps playing a trick on his neighbours by shouting, 'Wolf'. But he cried wolf so often that when a real wolf came and attacked his flock, nobody believed him and the sheep were killed. Crying wolf is raising a false alarm.

WHY DO WE SAY ...

FORLORN HOPE

The *verloren hoop*, being the Dutch for lost troop, were the body of men picked to lead a storming party, knowing their lives would probably be lost in the attack.

The first use of forlorn hope in the English language in the sixteenth century also described them as the troop going first into battle and falling to make a passage for the rest. Forlorn hope came to indicate any perilous or desperate enterprise.

WHY DO WE SAY ...

SAVE FACE

The English community living in China in the nineteenth century were struck by the elaborate methods employed by the Chinese to avoid giving or receiving humiliation.

The English somewhat mistakenly called this saving face, though what the Chinese were worried about was *tiu lien*, which means losing face. Nonetheless, saving face means avoiding disgrace or embarrassment.

WHY DO WE SAY ...

GO FROM PILLAR TO POST

This is a very old phrase, and when first used in the fifteenth century it was the other way round: going from post to pillar.

Its origin lies in the first games of tennis, which began in the cloisters of the old monasteries. Early illustrations show the players patting a ball back and forth with the bare hand in the courtyard formed by the posts and pillars that held up the roof of the surrounding cloisters. The ball may well have been bounced off these in the early games because nets and rackets did not develop till later.

John Lydgate, a Benedictine monk and friend of Chaucer, wrote a poem in 1420 that said, 'Thus from post to pillar he was made to dance.' By the sixteenth century, people started saying from pillar to post when they meant someone was harassed from one place or predicament to another.

WHY DO WE SAY ...

IN A PRETTY PICKLE

This saying comes from the Dutch words *in de pekel zitten*, sitting in the pickle, which was literally the brine or vinegar in which food was placed to preserve it.

When people began using the phrase in the sixteenth century to indicate a sorry plight, they said ill pickle. But these days we say pretty pickle or fine pickle to add emphasis to the mess.

WHY DO WE SAY ...

LAME DUCK

The Stock Exchange is well known for having bull and bear markets, but in earlier times it also had lame ducks, people who could not pay up on settlement day to cover the bargains they had struck.

David Garrick, one of England's greatest actors, coined the phrase in a play that he wrote in 1771: 'Change Alley bankrupts waddle out [like] lame ducks.'

During the convoys of World War II, torpedoed ships that were still afloat but unable to keep up with the other ships' speed were also called lame ducks. So are American office holders who fail or do not seek re-election but still have some months left in office until a new candidate takes over. Whether a person or an object, a lame duck is disabled or ineffectual.

Why do we say ...

Spitting image

The spitting image is an exact likeness and came from seventeenth-century folk who would say of their father, for example, that we are 'as like him as if spit out of his mouth'.

The old form was spittan or spitten, even the spit and image. Now it's easier to say as 'spitting image'.

WHY DO WE SAY ...

NAMBY-PAMBY

English poet Ambrose Philips wrote some sickly sentimental rhymes to flatter the daughters of influential friends. He called one child 'dimply damsel, sweetly smiling'. Another he described as 'timely blossom, infant fair'.

Some of his contemporaries in the eighteenth century took exception to the infantile odes and satirically twisted Ambrose's name into Namby-pamby, making it a byword for feeble childishness.

Philips, stung by being mocked, hung up a rod at the coffee house he frequented, threatening to use it on Alexander Pope, one of his main critics. But Pope kept his criticism verbal because Philips was also a skilled swordsman!

WHY DO WE SAY ...

SHOW A LEG

Some ships in the British navy used to allow women aboard. A few wives were even aboard in battle, carrying gunpowder and bandaging the wounded. They had the privilege of getting an extra half-hour lying-in after the men got up to do the ship-board jobs.

In the morning, the officer would call out, 'Show a leg'. All those with hairy legs in the hammocks had to get up. The curvaceous female ones could stay where they were. It's not quite like that today, but show a leg still means get a move on.

WHEN MY SHIP COMES IN

Merchants who put up the money for the nineteenth-century trading ships to sail the seas to buy exotic cargoes from foreign lands were always waiting for their ship to come in.

If the ship returned safely from its hazardous journey, they would make a lot of money from the sale of the cargo. The phrase became synonymous with making a fortune.

WHY DO WE SAY ...

BEE IN THE BONNET

In olden times, a muddled person was described as having bees in the brain because of the straightforward analogy to having too many ideas buzzing around the head.

English poet Robert Herrick took the idea forward with a popular poem in 1648 called *The Mad Maid's Song*. The obsessed maiden cries, 'For pity, Sir, find out that bee, which bore my love away. I'll seek him in your bonnet brave, I'll seek him in your eyes.' A bee in the bonnet then entered currency as being obsessed with an idea.

WHY DO WE SAY . . .

WHAT A FIASCO

Although a fiasco now means any disastrous failure, the word started
out as specifically applying to a theatre performance which flopped.

It comes from the Italian *far fiasco* – to make a flask – and meant
to break down during a performance. Various incidents involving a
flask in Italian theatrical history have been labelled as the origin,
including a clown who blamed the flask he was using as a stage prop
for failing to raise any laughs.

WHY DO WE SAY ...

DOG IN THE MANGER

In one of Aesop's fables, a dog stations itself in a manger and stops the oxen and horses from eating the hay although it has no use for the fodder itself.

Thus, a churlish person who grudges others using something he does not want for himself is described as 'dog in the manger'.

WHY DO WE SAY...

HALCYON DAYS

In Greek legend, Halcyone throws herself into the sea on learning in a dream that her husband, King Ceyx, has drowned in a storm. The gods are struck by her grief and transform the couple into kingfishers so that they can live happily as birds of the water.

As an extra boon, they and their descendants are promised that whenever they are hatching their eggs, on a nest of fishbones floating in the water, the seas will be untroubled by storms for fourteen days.

Although kingfishers nest on land beside streams, not floating at sea as the ancients thought, halcyon came to mean contentment and halcyon days a special period of calm, which the Greeks allocated to fourteen days during the winter solstice.

WHY DO WE SAY ...

HOODLUM

A reporter in nineteenth-century San Francisco wanted to write about a gang of street criminals led by a man called Muldoon. To escape reprisal, he spelled the name backwards as Noodlum, but a printer on the paper used an 'H' by mistake and produced Hoodlum.

This is the favourite story for the origin of the slang word for gangster. Some sticklers claim that they cannot find the story about Noodlum or Hoodlum in the old newspaper files, but let them come up with a better one!

WHY DO WE SAY ...

IN THE LIMELIGHT

Captain Thomas Drummond, a British army engineer in the 1820s, invented an intense white light produced by heating a piece of lime, in order to improve his map surveying capabilities in murky weather.

Drummond used his limelight for markers which could easily be observed in dull conditions when measuring distances by triangulation for map making. The scientific world welcomed his invention and started applying it to other uses, including lighthouses and theatrical lighting, where the leading actors found themselves in the full glare of bright light. Anyone in the limelight came to be in the focus of public interest.

WHY DO WE SAY . . .

GO THROUGH THE HOOP

One of the most famous circus tricks, still popular after two centuries, is to jump through a hoop of blazing fire on horseback. The bareback rider can also vault from the horse, bursting through a paper hoop to land again on its back.

Fewer people go to the circus now to witness these feats, but going through the hoop became the equivalent of undergoing a trial or ordeal.

WHY DO WE SAY . . .

PIG IN THE MIDDLE

Pig in the middle was a rough-and-tumble children's game in which one child was encircled by others and had to escape them. In the gentler version, the pig in the middle has to intercept a ball thrown between the others.

Thus a person likened to the game is someone who is stuck unenviably between opposing groups of people.

WHY DO WE SAY ...

NOT WORTH THE RUSH

This saying comes from such early medieval times that no one knows for certain if it refers to the tallowed rush used for lighting or to the fresh green rushes which were strewn on the floor for important visitors as the original welcome mat.

Whether rush light or rush floor, the visitor not worth a rush was of no importance. Since the custom of using rushes is long forgotten, we equally use the phrase these days for articles of no value where once it only applied to people.

WHY DO WE SAY . . .

TALK TURKEY

Turkeys were originally wild fowl in North America and the story goes that a white settler went hunting with a Red Indian and tried to cheat him in dividing the spoil by keeping all the turkeys and giving the Indian all the buzzards.

By the 1820s, talking turkey meant speaking frankly or getting down to the hard facts, though Americans never developed the other side of the coin, talking buzzard, which presumably would have been to talk deceitfully.

WHY DO WE SAY ...

THE MOMENT OF TRUTH

The moment of truth comes directly from the Spanish *el momento de la verdad*, the point in the bull fight when the matador makes the final sword thrust.

Ernest Hemingway wrote about it in his widely read novel *Death in the Afternoon* in 1932, making outsiders aware that the Spanish described this end to the bull fight as the moment of truth. It came to mean any turning point or time of revelation.

QUEER THE PITCH

The pitch was a market stall where goods were traded, often by a 'pitcher' who made up a story about each article he was offering.

Rivals or disbelievers would sometimes interfere and spoil the story, or 'queer' it as they used to say. Hence queering the pitch was the same as spoiling a sale, or spoiling things in general, as the meaning spread.

WHY DO WE SAY ...

CURRY FAVOUR

This has nothing to do with eating curry and originally had very little to do with favour because the original fifteenth-century saying was to curry favel.

In those days the only currying that went on was to curry, or groom, a horse. The act of stroking the horse down came to be associated with flattery or blandishments. Favel was the name of a chestnut horse, presumably a showy one that was not as reliable or good as he appeared, because currying favel meant using insincere flattery. Favel has passed out of equine history and instead we regard humans who curry favour as ingratiating themselves.